BIRDS
OF LODI GARDEN

With its undulating swards of green, groves of grand old trees, clumps of flowering bushes, majestic old monuments and zig-zag watercourse, Lodi Garden attracts more than fifty species of birds, several of which have made their homes here, others which visit when the season and mood suits them. Most early morning and evening walkers appear to be in far too much of a hurry to appreciate its avian inhabitants, and are surprised when told there are so many types of birds waiting to be seen and heard. All you really have to do is keep your ears cocked and to stand and stare... The birds here have been listed in order of their scientific 'rollcall'. The common English name is followed by the scientific name and the Hindi name in the following manner:

ENGLISH NAME
Scientific name HINDI NAME

1 BLACKRUMPED FLAMEBACK

Dinopium benghalense

SONERA KATPHORA

A flamboyant myna-sized woodpecker, with a 'bottlebrush' crest, gold-and-black back, and streaked greyish white breast. It may clamp itself on a tree-trunk close to you with a gleeful ringing cackle and then scuttle round the trunk as if to play peek-a-boo, or run up and down in clockwise spurts as it hunts insects. Its undulating flight is often accompanied by that lunatic call.

2 BROWNHEADED BARBET

Megalaima zeylanica BADA BASANTHA

A grass-green myna-sized bird, difficult to spot, with an oversized yellow ochre bill and a brown (stippled with white) face, neck and upper back. Its loud, incessant 'kutroo-kutroo' call is a dead give-away, and you may winkle one out of a fruiting peepul or bakain (Persian lilac). Especially fond of summer, and nests in neat round holes excavated in tree trunks and thick branches.

3 COPPERSMITH BARBET

Megalaima haemacephala CHHOTA BASANTHA

A sparrow- sized dumpy green bird with a face like a clown in crimson, yellow, black and white. Large, soulful dark eyes, a bristly moustache and a delightful hiccupping 'tok-tok-tok' call emitted while standing on tiptoe, complete the character sketch. Summer-loving and frugivorous, it too nests in neat round holes excavated in soft wood.

4 INDIAN GREY HORNBILL

Ocyceros birostris

DHAND, DHAMAR, DHANESH, DHANEL, CHALOTRA, LAMDAR

A large (kite-sized, with longer tail) unmistakable shabby grey bird with a long downcurving bill with a 'casque' on top, and long dangly graduated grey-and-white tail that looks as though it is about to fall off. Big old neem and peepul trees are favourite courting and nesting places and their metallic mewling calls are often heard from the trees near the boundary of the India International Center.

5 COMMON HOOPOE

Upupa epop

HUDHUD

Most often mistaken for a woodpecker, this is that raw silk and zebra-striped bird (about myna-sized), with a slim curving needle-like bill, that can be seen trundling about on the grass tending the turf assiduously (picking up worms and insects), and expanding its beautiful Japanese fan-crest from time to time as if in astonishment. Its call is a soft pleasant, 'Hud-hud-hud'.

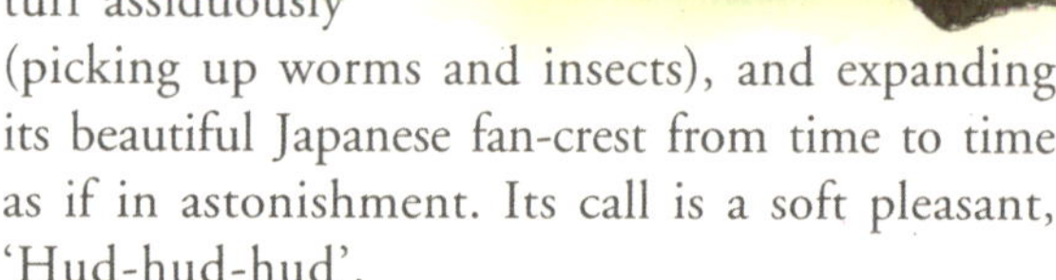

6 WHITETHROATED KINGFISHER

Halcyon smyrensis

KILKILA

In brilliant turquoise, chocolate brown and dazzling white, this kingfisher is hard to miss as it eyeballs you with a wolfish grin from its perch, its large scarlet broadsword bill ever ready! Often found well away from water, as it subsists happily on insects, small reptiles and frogs, this myna-sized kingfisher has a ringing 'kililil' call and a cackle of laughter, often given on the wing.

7 GREEN BEE-EATER

Merops orientalis

PATRINGA

Slim, elfin green and masked, with a head that look burnished saffron in the sun and with pin-feathers in the tail like twin antennae. Green bee-eaters may occasionally be seen skating over the lawns and high above the tombs, snapping up dragonflies and bees and emitting trilling notes as they do. March and September appear to be favourite months for these birds.

8 ASIAN KOEL

Eudynamys scolopacea KOEL

The male is slinky black, narrow-waisted, with lurid red eyes, and a little longer than the crow. The female, stippled in brown and white, resembles dappled branches and twigs. As summer approaches, their maniacal 'Kuoo-kuoo-kuoo!' calls get increasingly insistent as plans are put into place to diddle the crows in whose nests they will deposit their eggs. They can be seen flying across the gardens in unseemly haste as the subterfuge is discovered (usually too late), or while males chase each other while courting. Summer and monsoons are the prime time for them.

9 PLUMHEADED PARAKEET

Psittacula cyanocephala TUYIA TOTA

Their shrill questioning 'toooi? toooi?'call is the best indicator of their presence. A little smaller than the Roseringed parakeet, the males have a plum-coloured head and bluish collar; females have grey heads. The bill is papaya orange.

10 ALEXANDRINE PARAKEET

Psittacula eupatria

HIRAMAN TOTA

Larger and slower flying than the more common Rose-ringed parakeet, the Alexandrine wears maroon epaulettes, has a hoarser voice (Keeak! Kee-ah!), and a powerful red nut-cracker bill. Small groups may be heard calling from tall trees. Their domed heads and bulging eyes give them a charmingly mad-scientist expression.

11 ROSERINGED PARAKEET

Psittacula krameri TOTA

The shrill chillie-sharp parakeet that streaks about everywhere, and which comes down to the various feeding-spots in the garden for breakfast. Only males wear the smart rose-pink collar around their necks. They nest in holes in tree trunks and branches and in old buildings.

12 HOUSE SWIFT

Apus affinus ABABEEL, BABEELA

These tiny (smaller than sparrow) fastback winged birds are sooty-brown with a white band across the rump and a squared-off tail, and can be seen zipping in and out of the tombs in the gardens, or zooming over their domes, chasing insects.

13 SPOTTED OWLET

Athene brama ULLOO

One of the gardens' most enchanting inhabitants, these dumpy brown owls with their icing-sugar-dusted heads will glare at you out of round golden eyes, from outside a tree-trunk hollow, and bob their heads in disbelief. The groves of big trees in the gardens, especially those abutting the IIC are sure places to spot these owlets, even during the day. Their querulous 'chrr! churr! chevak!' calls, especially towards dusk, is another sure indicator of their presence.

14 ROCK PIGEON

Columba livia

KABUTAR

The familiar blue-grey pigeon with its iridescent head and orange eyes, is wonderfully promiscuous. They can be pretty quarrelsome too.

15 LAUGHING DOVE

Streptopelia senegalensis CHHOTA FAKTA

The small (one size smaller than myna) demure sandstone and grey dove with a small 'chessboard' pattern on the either side of its neck. Comes down at feeding-spots, and can calm your jangled nerves with its soothing 'Coo-roo-roo' call.

16 EURASIAN COLLARED DOVE

Streptopelia decaocto FAKHTA

The plump pale fawn dove, with a black half-collar, which looks as though it has been too generous with talcum powder! A frequent visitor to feeding-spots, it eats seriously, bobbing its head up and down., Females often valiantly chase crows, which seem to have developed a taste for their eggs or chicks.

17 YELLOWFOOTED GREEN PIGEON

Treron phoenicoptera

HARIAL

If you hear a strange wheezy, chortling call, look up and scan the trees carefully. With their greenish-yellow plumage, green pigeons are masters of camouflage, and will sit tight watching you. Their heads and necks are grey, they have chrome-yellow legs and a lilac patch on their shoulders, and love the leafy reaches of neem and peepul trees. However, they enjoy sunning themselves from bare branches in the early morning or late evening, so that is when to check them out.

18 REDWATTLED LAPWING

Vanellus indicus

TITIRI

An upright-standing, bronze brown plover, with long yellow legs, black head and neck and snow white undersides, and blood-red wattles near the eyes, this is the bird with the shrill, 'did-ye-do-it?' call. It can be seen occasionally strutting about on the lawns or in the watercourse. Can be heard from miles away.

19 SHIKRA

Accipiter badius SHIKRA

Its shrill 'ki-kee!' 'ki-ke!' call is again the best indicator of its presence, usually accompanied by

the alarm calls of other birds. A diminutive (between myna and crow sized) fierce-eyed hawk, males are bluish-grey, females (a little larger) more greyish-brown, both with a fine rufous weave across their breasts. Youngsters have horizontal stippling down their breasts. Usually wait in ambush in the trees and will dive out in a snaking swoop after other birds, which are hunted assiduously.

20 LITTLE CORMORANT

Phalacrocorax niger PAAN KAWWA

If the rains are good and the watercourse filled up, you may be rewarded by the sight of these sleek black (if stretched, crow sized!) birds swimming low and sinuously. Somewhat duck-like in profile, they have sharp hook- tipped bills, and stiff long tails, and the ability to dive under just as you focus on them. Some may 'crucify' themselves in order to dry out bedraggled wings; their feathers are not waterproof.

21 LITTLE EGRET

Egretta garzetta

KANCHIA BAGLA

This elegant satin-white heron, can be seen wading fastidiously in the watercourse, lifting its yellow-booted black feet carefully, as it hunts frogs and small fish. In the monsoons, it wears attractive lacy plumes on its head and breast.

22 INDIAN POND HERON

Ardeola grayii

BAGLA

This stocky brown heron with streaks down its neck and head, has blazing white wings and scaly yellow or greenish legs. Usually to be found at the edge of, or in, the watercourse. During the monsoons, the birds are outfitted in an attractive lacy maroon plumage. They will stand stock-still undetected and take off with an irritable croak when you come too close.

23 RUFOUS TREE PIE

Dendrocitta vagabunda

MAHLAT

In shape rather crow-like (to which family it belongs) with a sooty black head and throat, brown, black, pale grey and white wings and a long silver grey tail, the presence of tree pies is best detected by the clear fluting, 'bobo-link' or 'ko-kila' call, often following by a harsh metallic grating and sardonic 'ta-chak, ta-chak' chorttle. Arboreal, and easily spotted flying across the gardens between groves.

24 BLACK KITE

Milvus migrans CHEEL

The large dark fork-tailed raptor that has stolen countless sandwiches and paranthas, from picnickers in the gardens. Usually circling overhead, they may come down to a fresh-watered section of lawn for a drink and a bath.

25 HOUSE CROW

Corvus spendens KAWWA

Needs no introduction. Their numbers in the garden appear directly proportional to the amount of garbage strewn by picnickers and visitors. Large gangs also come to the feeding spots. Sometimes accompanied by larger, all jet-black large-billed crows (*Corvus macrohynchos*).

26 EURASIAN GOLDEN ORIOLE

Oriolus oriolus

PEELAK

A summer visitor arriving by April, this beautiful if effete yellow and black bird with its red bill can take your breath away. Listen for a lovely fluting 'Peela-we-o' call and look carefully in the neems, where the birds like to nest.

27 RED THROATED FLYCATCHER

Ficedula parva

TARRA

A winter visitor, this tiny (smaller than a sparrow) brown bird with its round head and round eyes and droopy wings wears a flare of orange on its breast (males only) and tosses restlessly after insects. Best spotted during October and November, and then again in March and April when many pass through the capital to and from their wintering haunts elsewhere.

28 GREY-HEADED CANARY FLYCATCHER

Culicicapa ceylonensis ZIRD PHUTKI

Another diminutive flycatcher that spends the winter with us, this one is attractive in grey and sulphur. Its shrill 'Chick-wichee-wichee' song may be familiar to regular visitors to Himalayan hillstations, where it is a summer resident. The casuarina groves and areas around the watercourse are favourite haunts.

29 ORIENTAL MAGPIE ROBIN

Copsychus saularis

DHAYAL

The smart, bright-eyed black-and -white bird whose beautiful fluting sonatas greet early morning walkers to the gardens especially in spring and summer. Also capable of a harsh churring (when reviews are bad!), this attractive bird can often be seen singing from perches high in the trees. Females are ash-grey and white.

30 BLACK REDSTART

Phoenicurus ochruros THITHIRI

A winter visitor, the male has a silver-grey head, charcoal face, neck and back, and rich rufous belly, underside and tail. The female is biscuit brown with a touch of rufous under the tail. Quiet and demure, redstarts have an endearing habit of bowing and shivering their tails as they flit down from branches to the ground.

Arrive by September and leave by the end of April.

31 BRAHMINY STARLING

Sturnus pagodarum

BRAHMINI MYNA

A smart grey-and-fawn myna with a sleek black head and recumbent crest, which is raised hilariously when the bird is excited or besotted. Saunter around in pairs or small parties, often with other mynas. It has a pleasant song, delivered with oodles of emotion, with head thrown back, especially in spring.

32 INDIAN MYNA

Acridotheres tristis

MYNA

Apart from the House crow, the other dada bird of the gardens. Large congregations of these coffee-brown birds can be seen arguing noisily on the lawns, and occasionally indulging in all-out wresting bouts. Their heads are glossy black, offset by a yellow eye-patch, bills and legs, and a white patch on the wings, prominent in flight.

33 ASIAN PIED STARLING

Sturnus contra ABLAK MYNA

An earnest looking black-and-white myna with a papaya-orange patch of bare skin in front of the eyes and similarly coloured bill and legs. Can be seen on the lawns, especially after they have been watered. These seemingly self-effacing mynas can create a racket at dusk, when large numbers congregate to roost in trees and thickets.

34 RED-VENTED BULBUL

Pycnonotus cafer

BULBUL

This dusky brown bulbul (smaller than the myna), with its black head and truncated chest , and crimson vent, is a familiar pugnacious inhabitant of the gardens, and will join the parakeets, doves and crows at the feeding spots. It has a pleasant mellifluous call.

35 RED-WHISKERED BULBUL

Pycnonotus jocosus SIPAHI BULBUL

Slimmer than the above, with a more jaunty crest, this brown (above) and white(below)bulbul with its chin-straps and crimson cheek-patches does indeed look like a palace guardsman. Sweeter voiced than the above, it is less common and usually driven away by its bullying and more bohemian relative.

36 ASHY PRINIA

Prinia socialis

KALI PHUTKI

A tiny (smaller than sparrow) sleek bird, steely grey above (which turns reddish brown in winter) and off-white below, with a long graduated tail that is constantly flicked up and down, the Ashy prinia skulks at the bottom of hedges and flowering bushes picking up insects, emitting a warning 'tee-tee-tee' call if you come too close. A good bird to look out for when you're taking time out on a bench – just scan the base of the nearest hedge or flowerbed.

37 ORIENTAL WHITE EYE

Zosterops palpebrosus

BABOONA

Easier heard than seen. White eyes have a soft jingling call, which can often be heard as you walk past the groves of trees. Neem seems to be an especial favourite. Sparrow-sized, the birds are olive-yellow and off-white and sport white 'monocles', giving them a solemn look. They find bottlebrush flowers irresistable. Usually move around in small parties.

38 LESSER WHITETHROAT

Sylvia curruca

Anytime between September and April you are likely to hear an irritable 'tch-tch-tch' as you walk beneath the trees in the gardens. The perpetrator is the Lesser whitethroat, a small (smaller than a sparrow) beige-brown (above) and creamy-white (below) bird, with a neat grey cap and white cheeks, assiduously hunting insects and caterpillars amongst the foliage. Be tolerant of its apparent misanthropy- it may have flown all the way down from Siberia to be here.

39 TAILORBIRD

Orthotomus sutorius

DARZEE

The famous leaf sewing tinytot (smaller than a sparrow) with a megaphone voice! Olive green, with a saffron cap and long graduated tail, flicked up and down constantly, the tailorbird advertises its presence with its loud 'towit-towit-towit' or 'chewit-chewit-chewit' call. Hedges, flowering bushes and trees are favourite haunts, and broad-leaved foliage is preferred for nesting.

40 LARGE GREY BABBLER

Turdoides malcolmi SAT BHAI

If you hear loud, incessant and manic 'kay-kay-kay' calls emanating from the bottom of a hedge, or piles of leaf litter, look out for a gang of six or seven sandy grey birds, with hard pale yellow eyes, and ashy 'caste – marks' across their glowering foreheads. They will hop and canter and scuttle, and, if forced, fly weakly, flaring out white-edged tails as they try desperately not to crash-land. Large grey babblers hunt insects in the leaf-litter like cops looking for heroin.

41 JUNGLE BABBLER

Turdoides striatus SAT BHAI

Slightly smaller than the above, and more common, these 'brown paper' babblers look endearingly bad-tempered and untidily put together. They also move around in gangs of six and seven, and will hop and bounce menacingly towards all who threaten them. Also to be found turning up the dirt and leaf litter. Khaki brown all over with yellow eyes and legs.

42 PURPLE SUNBIRD

Nectarina asiatica

SHAKHAR KHORA

A tiny shrill iridescent midnight blue bird with a long curving needle bill. It zips amongst nectar-yielding flowers with all the panache of a popstar. Females are clad in dowdy ochre-yellow, and males turn to this colour usually between September and February, but with a purple necktie to distinguish them. Often mistakenly called 'hummingbirds'.

43 HOUSE SPARROW

Passer domesticus

GAURIYA

Needs no introduction, but appears to be getting scarcer all over Delhi, according to reports from residents in the city. Pugnacious, street –smart and savvy, it'll be a good idea to check out the feeding spots in the garden to see how they are doing here.

44 WHITE WAGTAIL

Motacilla alba DHOBIN

A plump ash-grey, white and black winter visitor that saunters about the lawns like a landlord, wagging its tail up and down as if in approval. Arrives by around September and leaves by April. Dipping flight usually accompanied by a high-pitched squeak.

FAVOURITE HOTSPOTS

Like us, birds too have their favourite hotspots even in the gardens, where we are more likely to meet them. Holes and hollows in tree trunks or branches provide homes for flamebacks,. barbets, hornbills, parakeets, owlets, magpie robins, starlings and mynas, and so are hot property and worth checking out.

The leafy reaches of trees provide sanctuary to the likes of koels, doves, green pigeons, shikras, kingfishers, tree pies, house crows, golden orioles, flycatchers (usually lower down)bulbuls, white eyes and whitethroats.

Lawns, especially when freshly watered, are loved by crows, mynas, pigeons, doves, hoopoes, magpie robins, redstarts, wagtails and black kites. Undergrowth and leaf litter, as well as hedges and bushes, are patrolled by prinias , tailorbirds, bulbuls and babblers.

Trees or bushes in flower or with fruit will attract virtually the whole cast, though often sunbirds will steal the show at flowering plants.

The watercourse (when filled) is the haunt of cormorants, egrets, pond herons, and lapwings.

Look up at the sky for wheeling black kites, swifts and bee-eaters, which specialize in mid air meals.

The feeding areas are visited by crows, parakeets, pigeons, mynas, and when the crowds thin out, doves, magpie robins and babblers.

But do remember, all the birds in Lodi Gardens can fly...

NOTES

NOTES